creative cut cards

CREATIVE CUT CARDS

35 GREETING CARDS FOR EVERY OCCASION

LARK
New York

LARK
New York

An Imprint of Sterling Publishing
1166 Avenue of the Americas
New York, NY 10036

ISBN 978-1-4547-0930-5

Distributed in Canada by Sterling Publishing
c/o Canadian Manda Group, 664 Annette Street
Toronto, Ontario, Canada M6S 2C8
Distributed in the United Kingdom by GMC Distribution Services
Castle Place, 166 High Street, Lewes, East Sussex, England BN7 1XU
Distributed in Australia by Capricorn Link (Australia) Pty. Ltd.
P.O. Box 704, Windsor, NSW 2756, Australia

For information about custom editions, special sales, and premium and corporate purchases, please contact Sterling Special Sales at 800-805-5489 or specialsales@sterlingpublishing.com.

Photography by Chris Bain
Illustrations by Orrin Lundgren
Designed by Amy Trombat

Manufactured in China

2 4 6 8 10 9 7 5 3 1

larkcrafts.com

contents

Introduction

I love paper for the simplicity of its design: at its essence, paper is the ultimate minimalist, utilitarian tool. From napkins to notepads, we touch it every day—in situations as mundane as wiping a drip of coffee or as pivotal as the receipt of a college acceptance letter. The wonderful thing about paper is that despite its many forms, it always provides a platform for your ideas to shine!

Take advantage of the amazing new specialty papers hitting the shelves, from patterned to gradient, hardworking card stock to exuberant glitter, and create personalized, handmade cards. With *Creative Cut Cards*, thirty-five deceptively simple projects give you the tools to create cards as special and heartwarming as the words within them!

Turn to the Basic Instruction and Tools section (page ix) to learn about the simple tools needed to begin crafting. To begin, you need nothing more than a simple craft knife, a cutting mat, and paper. However, you might find it useful to expand your craft drawer to include a metal rule, carbon transfer paper, and more. For holidays and special occasions from graduations to weddings, turn to Celebrations (page 1). For special days like Valentine's Day, turn to Special Days (page 25). And for any day worthy of a greeting, find a selection of Blank Cards to customize (page 51).

Be creative and have fun!

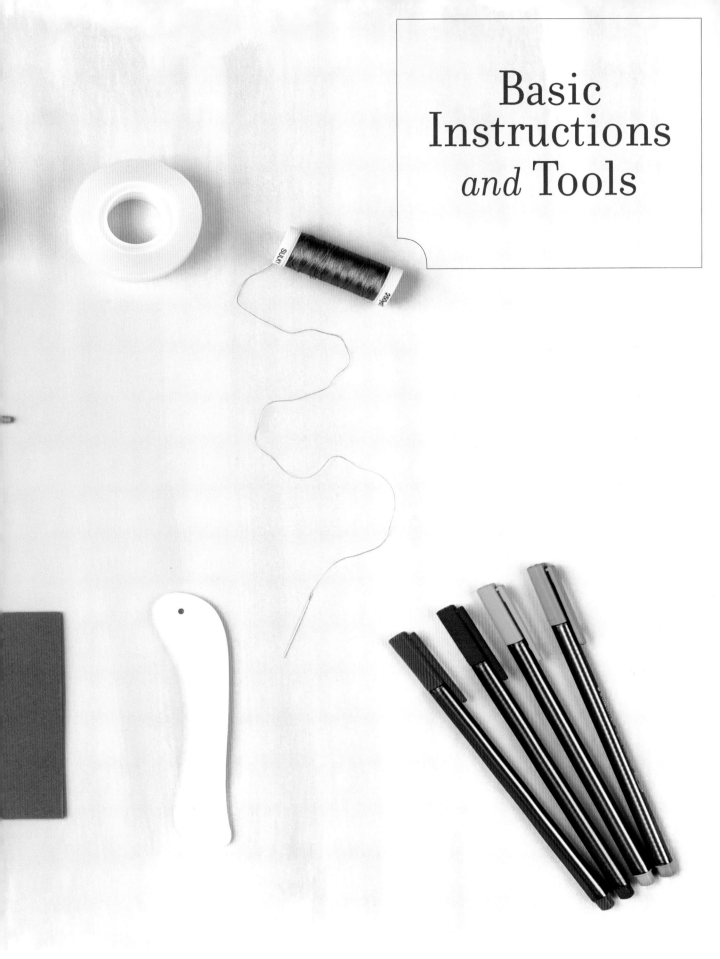

Basic Instructions *and* Tools

Paper

Card stock

Card stock is a thick, yet malleable, weight of paper that is standard for most card making. The thickness of card stock is measured in "points." We recommend 10–12 point for the projects in this book, but if you prefer thinner or thicker paper, any stock that will fold can be used.

Specialty Paper

When cutting stripes, windows, and shapes out of card stock, it can be fun to have specialty papers peek through. Texture, color, and shine can add a special element to paper projects. Some specialty papers used in this book include glitter paper, watercolor paper, velvet paper, vellum paper, and even standard copy paper.

Adhesive

Glue stick

Standard glue sticks are perfect for many paper-cutting projects: They deposit just the right amount of glue to adhere paper, without drips. Make sure to pick a clear-drying variety to avoid residues on your finished card.

PVA glue

PVA (polyvinyl acetate) glue is the standard white glue you might find in an elementary school classroom, and is also known as wood glue. PVA glue is perfect when you need more hold than a glue stick will provide. For extra control, use a small paintbrush to apply this adhesive.

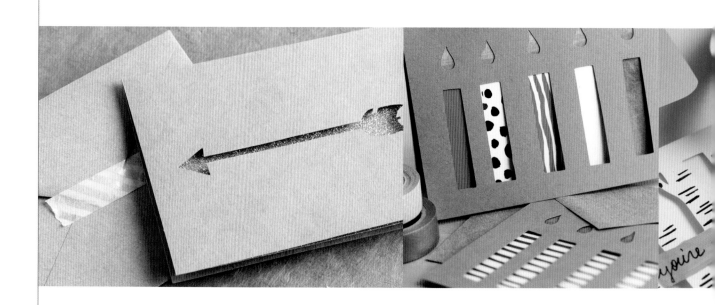

Adhesive dots

These sticky, premeasured dots of adhesive combine the convenience of tape with the strong hold of glue. In some cases, they can add dimensionality by subtly lifting elements on your card, creating a feeling of depth. There is no need to wait for these dots to dry, so they are perfect for last-minute crafting.

Double sided tape

Standard double-sided tape is a home-office staple that can neatly hold together cut paper. When used between layers of paper, it is completely invisible, and allows the paper to sit flush, creating no depth or gapping between elements.

Low-tack tape

Low-tack tape can be gently repositioned or removed, allowing you to make slight adjustments on your card until you are completely happy with an element's placement. This adhesive is great for cards-in-progress, but is rarely used in a final project, as it is not considered a permanent adhesive.

Transparent cellulose tape

Perfect for permanently joining paper, transparent cellulose tape is strong and clear. This easy-tear adhesive is available in many colors, but for paper crafts, the transparent variety is the most versatile.

Cutting Tools

Hole punch/shaped punches

You might be familiar with the hole punch as a standard office supply, perfect for preparing papers for three-ring binding. These easy-to-find tools can be used to create perfect small circles for crafting, but the size of your circle will be restricted. Shaped punches, available in most craft stores, allow you to create perfect, uniform shapes every time, perfect for cards like Many Adventures (page 22). They are available in many designs, from clouds to balloons to cupcakes!

Scissors/fringe scissors

For the projects in this book that require scissors for cutting, you can probably get away with a pair that you already own. However, a fresh, sharp pair of scissors will make your crafting go more smoothly and look more professional. If you are able to splurge, a sharp pair of craft scissors are a great investment. Novelty scissors, like the fringe scissors used in the Easter Egg Hunt card (page 38) make specialized tasks go more quickly.

Craft knife

A craft knife is the essential tool for detailed paper-cutting projects. It allows you to cut straight and curved lines, and to work with pencil-like precision. We recommend a #11 blade for the projects in this book.

Self-healing cutting mat

Your self-healing cutting mat will keep your counters free of scratches as you craft. Any size or shape will do, as long as your mat is large enough to fit your project in progress! Specialized craft mats are available in most craft stores.

Other

Vinyl eraser

Vinyl erasers are the essential tool for erasing pencil marks without damaging your paper's surface. Find them in most office-, craft- or art-supply shops. Some erasers are pink, some are white—their most important quality is their makeup. Make sure to get a true vinyl eraser instead of synthetic rubber or synthetic soy-based materials.

Markers

Some of the projects in this book call for markers meant for coloring the paper surfaces that will peek through your cutouts. While standard felt-tip markers will do in most cases, we love blendable translucent ink markers for their buildable color, which make shading and ombre effects easy to attain.

Scoring tool

A scoring tool allows you to create a neat crease in paper, priming the way for a perfect fold. This is especially helpful with thicker stocks of paper, which can be difficult to fold cleanly.

Transferring Templates

Layering Technique

Photocopy your template onto standard copy paper. Using low-tack tape, position and secure the template over the card blank, ensuring proper placement. Carefully cut through both the copy paper and the card stock. When the design is completely cut, remove the copy paper, and smooth any edges that need touching up.

Transfer Paper Technique

Photocopy your template onto standard copy paper, making sure to reverse the image. Working from the back of your card blank, place down a piece of carbon transfer, and cover it with your printed template, facing up. Use a scorer or a blunt, pointed tool to trace around the lines of the template, using enough pressure to transfer a carbon line onto your card. Remove the template and carbon paper, and cut along your lines. Remove any excess markings with a vinyl eraser. (This technique works best on cards that have inner backing paper, to cover any transfer lines.)

Stencil Technique

This technique requires a thick acetate sheet. Place your acetate over the desired template, and using a permanent marker, carefully trace around the image. Move the acetate to your cutting mat and cut out the image. When you are ready to transfer your template to your card, place your stencil over the card stock, and trace around it with a pencil. Cut out your pencil lines with a craft knife, and erase any leftover markings with a vinyl eraser. This technique is great for creating many cards at a time, perfect for invitations or thank-you notes for a large event. It is also useful for transferring templates onto either the inside or the outside of a card, as the image can be reversed easily by flipping over your stencil.

Lightbox Technique

This method works best with thinner card stock, and requires the availability of a lightbox. Copy your template onto a piece of copy paper. Place the template below the stock you plan to cut, ensuring that you can see your template clearly. Using a pencil, trace the lines visible underneath the card stock onto the card. Move the card stock to your cutting mat and cut out your image. Erase any leftover markings with a vinyl eraser. (Tutorials are available online to create your own lightbox using a smartphone and an acrylic storage box.)

celebrations

welcome to the world

The birth of a baby represents a wonderful beginning. Celebrate the little things with this adorable card! With options for either a girl or a boy, the card is well suited for any baby shower.

designed by **Louise Burgoyne**

1. Cut white card stock to 10 x 5 inches (254 x 127 mm) and score widthwise across the middle. Fold in half to create card blank.

2. Trace the templates for the baby onesie and socks onto the blue paper, the star onto white paper, and four clothespins onto the brown kraft paper using the transfer instructions on page xiii. Cut out all of your traced shapes.

3. Draw a line looping from the top left corner to the top right corner of the card. This will be the clothesline.

4. Glue the baby onesie and socks just below the clothesline. Glue and place the white star onto the center of the baby onesie. Glue the kraft paper clothespins to the top of each item you've added to the clothesline.

5. Draw an outline around the items in black pen. If you're tentative, draw your line in pencil first; and when you're happy with it, draw over the pencil line in black ink. Use an eraser to remove any pencil lines.

6. Letter "It's a Boy" onto the right hand corner or wherever you wish it to be on the card. If you aren't comfortable hand-lettering, use the provided template. To make an "It's a Girl" card, simply follow the instructions above but change the color of the baby onesie to pink, put a white heart in the center, and write "It's a Girl."

MATERIALS + TOOLS

Scissors

1 sheet white card stock

Pencil

1 sheet blue paper

1 sheet white paper

1 sheet brown kraft paper

PVA or any suitable paper glue

Fine-line black pen

Scoring tool

Finished card measures 5 x 5 inches (127 x 127 mm).

make a wish!

Let your creativity run wild with this candle-themed birthday card. Use black-and-white stripes for a fortieth birthday; modern mint candles for a sweet sixteen; or colorful polka dots for the little one in your life. The possibilities are limited only by your imagination.

designed by **Ashley Pahl**

1. Create a stencil by transferring and cutting out the template using a craft knife.

2. Cut the kraft card stock to measure 8 x 11 inches (203.2 x 279.4 mm). Score and fold the card stock in half widthwise, creating a card blank measuring 8 x 5½ inches (203.2 x 139.7 mm). Unfold.

3. On the bottom half of the unfolded card, transfer the template onto what will become the front of the card. Make sure the candle design is centered on the front flap of the card in a landscape orientation.

4. Use a craft knife and cutting mat to cut out the shape, following the drawn lines. Gently erase any leftover pencil markings with a vinyl eraser.

5. Refold the card along the previously established fold line.

6. Cut a 5¼ x 3.8-inch (133.35 x 96.52-mm) piece of white card stock. Use the candle template again to determine where the white card stock will show through the paper-cut candles. Use yellow and orange markers or paint to create a horizontal stripe of color to peek through the cutout candle flames. Create a colorful pattern of your choice for the space beneath the candles themselves. Before applying glue, make sure your hand-colored pattern will show through the candle cutouts correctly.

7. Apply a thin layer of glue to the top edge of the front of the patterned white card stock.

8. Adhere the patterned card stock to the inside top edge of the front flap of the card, near the crease, making sure that the stripes and patterns of color show through the correct cutouts on the front of the card. Allow glue to dry completely (about 10 minutes).

MATERIALS + TOOLS

Pencil

1 sheet kraft card stock

Craft knife with sharp blade

Vinyl eraser

Scissors

Self-healing cutting mat

Scoring tool

1 sheet white card stock

Yellow and orange markers or paint

Craft glue

Finished card measures 8 x 5½ inches (203.2 x 139.7 mm).

TIP: *Always wash hands before working with kraft card stock. Kraft card stock and paper are notorious for absorbing any little bit of grease or oil from hands and fingertips.*

bridal elegance

It is always so special to receive a card that was made by hand with you
in mind. Wow your wedding couple with this personalized, elegant,
handmade card. Feel free to customize your background
color to match the wedding's theme!

designed by **Brita Vallens**

1. Cut copy paper to measure 5 x 5 inches (127 x 127 mm).

2. Copy the card design template onto a piece of regular copy paper at full size.

3. Place the piece of paper with the copied template over the piece of white drawing paper.

> **TIP:** *To keep the template in place, cut it down a few inches smaller than the drawing paper and affix the corners of the template to the sketch paper with small pieces of tape. Your template will stay in place on the drawing paper as you cut, and you will be able to rotate both pieces without setting the template off while you work.*

4. Place the drawing paper—with the template in place on top—over the cutting mat. Using the craft knife, begin cutting along the lines of the template design. Take your time as you cut, and use a fair amount of pressure as you work to ensure that your cuts are making it through both the copy paper and the drawing paper.

> **TIP:** *If you have never worked with a craft knife before, consider practicing with a few scraps of the copy and drawing paper to become familiar with the movement of the knife and the weight of the papers before starting your final project.*

MATERIALS + TOOLS

Pencil

1 sheet copy paper

1 sheet white drawing paper

Craft knife

Self-healing cutting mat

Low-tack tape

Metal ruler

1 sheet kraft paper or card stock in a color of your choice (This project uses green.)

Bone scorer

Craft glue

Small paintbrush

Wax paper

Calligraphy pen in color of your choice

Finished card measures 6 x 5½ inches (152.4 x 139.7 mm).

5. Cut the entire design template with the craft knife. Start at one corner of the design and move around the edges and then spiral inward as you progress so you can be sure you are cutting the entire template. Check for missed cuts by running your hand over the template to feel for the grooves left by the craft knife. Use the tip of the craft knife to pop the cut pieces out of the template as you go.

6. When all of the template cuts have been made, carefully remove the design template from the drawing paper.

7. Use a metal ruler to cut the final border for the decorative piece, and use the craft knife to clean up any rough or inaccurate cuts in the design. After cutting your borders, a lacy white square will remain.

8. Cut an 11 x 6-inch (279.4 x 152.4-mm) size piece of kraft paper or card stock in a color of your choice. Fold the piece of paper in half and use a bone fold to sharpen the crease.

9. Brush a small amount of craft glue along the edges of the cut copy paper and position it in the center of the card's front flap.

10. Clean any excess glue with your finger or a paper towel and nestle the card between two sheets of wax paper before placing it between a stack of heavy books to dry (about 10 minutes).

11. Remove the card from the stack of books and make sure the card is completely dry before adding the couple's initials to the center circle of the decorative piece with a calligraphy pen, or glue a photo of the couple in the center.

> **TIP:** *If you choose to glue a picture to the center of the card, be sure to place the card between two clean sheets of wax paper and between the stack of books once the photo is glued in place to ensure that the card dries flat.*

celebrate love

This versatile and minimalist card is perfect for any wedding.
The card looks great in classic white, but if you're feeling fancy,
why not try colors to match the wedding's theme?

designed by **Sian Williams-Clarke**

1. Cut both pieces of white card stock to measure 10 x 7 inches (254 x 177.8 mm). Score and fold both pieces of stock widthwise, creating two card blanks measuring 5 x 7 inches (127 x 177.8 mm). Set one piece of card stock aside.

2. Reverse the template image and trace on to inside of card.

3. Cut out the template using a craft knife and cutting mat, working from the inside of the card.

4. Cut a square of colored paper, ensuring that it is large enough to completely cover the cut-out design, about 5 x 5 inches (127 x 127 mm).

5. Right side up, glue around the edges of the pearlescent backing paper and affix over the cut out design on inside of card.

> **TIP:** *Avoid gluing the middle of the pearlescent paper as this will show through the cutout of the card.*

6. Glue around the edges and center of the white card stock and affix to inner front of card, completely obscuring the pearlescent paper, and ensuring card is lined up with outer white card stock so that edges do not overhang. You are pasting one piece of card stock inside the other, creating a lining.

MATERIALS + TOOLS

2 sheets white card stock

Pencil

Craft knife

Self-healing cutting mat

Scissors

1 sheet colored or pearlescent paper

Scoring tool

Glue stick

Finished card measures 5 x 7 inches (127 x 177.8 mm).

pop your cork!

There are few days as exciting as January 1. It is full of excitement and the promise of a fresh new year to come. A bottle of champagne is often on the menu! Welcome a sparkling New Year with this champagne-themed New Year's card.

designed by **Louise Burgoyne**

1. Cut a 5 x 10-inch (127 x 254-mm) piece of white card stock. Score widthwise down the middle of the card stock and fold in half to create blank card.

2. Trace the bottle template onto the green paper and cut out. Repeat for the label template on yellow paper and for the label markings on black paper. Copy and cut out the Champagne spray using the pale blue paper. If you are in a rush or don't want to use the template, you can hand draw the spray onto the card at the end of the project.

3. Start by gluing the green bottle onto the left bottom corner of the front of the card. Allow time for the glue to dry (about 10 minutes). Once dry, glue the label on the bottle then glue the black marking on to the label. Finally, add the Champagne spray onto the card by gluing it in place (or drawing the spray by hand). You can use the template as your guide for placement of each part of the spray.

4. Write your greeting on the right bottom of the card.

5. Using a black fine-tip pen, draw an outline around each part of the bottle and spray for that extra-special finishing touch. (If you want to make the card more personal, add your name and the year to the label.)

MATERIALS + TOOLS

Scissors
1 sheet white card stock
Pencil
1 sheet green paper
1 sheet yellow paper
1 sheet pale blue paper
1 sheet black paper
PVA or any other paper glue
Scoring tool
Fine-line black pen

Finished card measures 5 x 5 inches (127 x 127 mm).

hugs & kisses

On occasions both happy and sad, our instinct is often to reach out
and hug our loved ones. For the times when a hug isn't possible, this card
is the next best thing. "XOXO" is the classic stand-in for hugs and kisses,
for any time that you wish you could give an in-person embrace.

designed by **Mia Yoshihara-Bradshaw**

1. Using a paper cutter, cut white card stock to 8 x 5 ½ inches (203.2 x 139.7 mm). Score widthwise and fold in half, creating a 5½ x 4-inch (139.7 x 101.6-mm) card.

2. Using a paper cutter, cut the red card stock to 8 x 5½ inches (203.2 x 139.7 mm). Trim the shorter edges slightly so that the stock is just smaller than the white card stock, about 7.9 x 5.4.inches (200.66 mm x 137.16 mm). Score widthwise and fold in half. Set aside.

3. Unfold the white card stock and lay on the cutting mat. Transfer the XOXO template to the front flap of the card, making sure that the template is centered.

4. Using a craft knife, cut out the template. Cut out the smaller details first and work your way up to the larger cutouts.

5. "XOXO" should now be on the front flap of card. Apply double-sided tape just below the inner fold so that you can attach the red inner card.

6. Position the red inner card within the white card stock, ensuring that the creases align.

7. Apply the red inner card to the double-sided tape by pressing firmly.

8. Flip the card over and fold. Place the card under heavy weight such as a thick book to help the card lay flat.

MATERIALS + TOOLS

Guillotine paper cutter

1 sheet white card stock

1 sheet red card stock

Self-healing cutting mat

Craft knife

Scoring tool

Double-sided tape

Finished card measures 4 x 5½ inches (101.6 x 139.7 mm).

conGRADulations

Graduations are always bittersweet moments of pride. Whether your loved one is graduating from Kindergarten or a doctoral program, the joy that accompanies a cap and tassel is infinite. Celebrate your favorite grad with this lighthearted card.

designed by **Louise Burgoyne**

1. Cut a 5 x 10-inch (127 x 254-mm) piece of white card stock. Score widthwise down the middle of the card stock and fold in half.

2. Trace the top and bottom of the mortarboard template onto the black paper using the pencil. Cut out both pieces.

3. Trace the ribbon template onto of the red paper or use the school's color to make it more personal. Cut out all the shapes.

4. Using the black pen, copy the greeting "conGRADulations!" onto the card blank. The entire word should be about half an inch (12.7 mm) from the bottom of the card.

5. Glue together the mortarboard, following the guide on the template. Place it in the center of the card, leaving an inch gap on either side. Place at any angle you want; then add the ribbon.

6. Using the black pen, draw the detail on the ribbon. Add details to the mortarboard with the white or silver pen.

MATERIALS + TOOLS

Scissors

1 sheet white card stock

Pencil

Mortatboard template

1 sheet black paper

Ribbon template

1 sheet red paper or school color of your choosing

Fine-line black pen

PVA or any other paper glue

Scoring tool

White or silver pen

Finished card measures 5 x 5 inches (127 x 127 mm).

a woven greeting

Intricate details weave paper together with a sweet message!
We used this fun card to celebrate Father's Day, but you can
write in any greeting to fit the celebration of your choice!

designed by **Amanda Sueiro Rier**

1. Cut the white card stock to 5½ x 8½ inches (139.7 x 215.9 mm). Score the stock widthwise and fold, creating a card measuring 5½ x 4¼ inches (139.7 x 114.3 mm).

2. Transfer template A to the front flap of the card, making sure that the template is centered. Using a craft knife and the cutting mat, cut out the four horizontal rectangles of the template and the Father's Day text, if desired. You can also hand letter a greeting onto the center panel of the card. Set aside.

3. Take the teal sheet of paper and cut out four strips that are roughly ¼ inch x 5½ inches (6.35 x 139.7 mm). Cut another strip that is ½ inch x 5½ inches (12.7 x 139.7 mm). Set aside.

4. From the green card stock, cut out ten strips measuring ⅛ inch x 5½ inches (3.175 x 139.7 mm) each. Set aside.

5. Cut the navy card stock into a 4¼ x 5½-inch (107.95 x 139.7-mm) rectangle. Set aside.

6. Open the white card stock card so that you are looking at the inside of the front flap. Place each teal strip over one of the rectangular cutouts on the front flap, adhering each with the glue pen. Glue the ½-inch (12.7-mm) teal strip in the middle of the card, covering the cutout text. If you have chosen to hand-letter a greeting, there is no need for the ½-inch (12.7-mm) teal strip.

7. Now the fun part! You are going to weave the ten green strips through the card starting at the bottom and ending up near the fold. Start from the inside of the card and work in an under over weave (weaving over the teal strips you just glued down). Repeat this step with the remaining nine

green strips. Once you are done, space them evenly. You may want to draw small pencil dots on the inside of the card to adhere the strips to the proper spots.

8. Take the fine-point glue pen and glue the tips of the strips down. (A toothpick works well to apply pressure to help secure the bond). Start closest to the fold and then move down and glue the other side.

9. Once you've finished gluing the strips, apply glue all around the inner front flap of the card. The pens work well for this because you can get every small area. Place glue around each inner edge of the card and adhere the navy 4¼ x 5½-inch (107.95 x 139.7-mm) sheet of card stock. Apply pressure.

MATERIALS + TOOLS

Scissors

1 sheet white card stock

Pencil

Craft knife

Self-healing cutting mat

Three sheets different colored card stock (This project used navy, teal, and green.)

Glue pen

Toothpick

Scoring tool

Finished card measures 4¼ x 5½ inches (107.95 x 139.7 mm).

festive bunting

This is the perfect project for using up scrap pieces of card stock to make a simple but unique handmade card. The colorful bunting is a cheery enough for birthdays, housewarmings, and all manner of festive celebrations!

designed by **Margaret Beagle**

1. Cut kraft card stock to measure 8 x 6 inches (203.2 x 152.4 mm). Score card stock widthwise, down the middle. Fold to create blank card and set aside.

2. Select colored card stock of your choice and cut with scissors into strips measuring approximately ¾ inch (19.1 mm) wide.

2. After cutting the strips, use scissors to cut the strips into small triangles. It's ok if each triangle isn't identical.

3. Once the triangles are cut, lay them out on the blank kraft card to create a garland with a swoop that you like. You can even use a pencil to mark where you want the triangles to go.

4. Glue the triangles down, making three garlands across the card. Once the glue has dried (about 10 minutes), run each garland through a sewing machine, stitching at the tops of each. Cut any excess thread.

TIP: *Make sure to test your sewing machine on a piece of scrap card stock to ensure that your tension is appropriate for sewing through paper.*

MATERIALS + TOOLS

1 sheet kraft brown card stock

Scissors

Card stock in colors of your choice (red, orange, yellow, green, and purple were used for this project), one sheet per color

Craft glue

Scoring tool

Sewing machine

Finished card measures 4 x 6 inches (101.6 x 152.4 mm).

many adventures

Lift your spirits with this cheerful, multicolored bunch of three-dimensional balloons! Using only solid card stock and a few simple tools you can create a vibrant, textured card fit for all celebrations.

designed by **Margaret Beagle**

1. Cut the kraft card stock to measure 10 x 7 inches (254 x 177.8 mm). Score and fold the card stock in half widthwise, creating a card blank measuring 5 x 7 inches (127 x 177.8 mm). Unfold.

2. Cut the white card stock to measure 3¾ x 4¼ inches (95.25 x 107.95 mm). This will leave a ¼-inch (6.35-mm) margin along each edge when glued on top of the front flap of the kraft card stock.

3. Using the template, trace three balloons of each color. Gently fold each balloon in half.

4. Using one cutout of each color, stack the balloons using glue only on the center of each balloon so the edges can be folded out.

5. Once the glue has dried, gently pull up each layer, creating a three dimensional effect. Repeat this three times to create three balloons.

6. To assemble, adhere the white card stock on to the folded kraft notecard. Adhere each balloon to the white card stock.

MATERIALS + TOOLS

1 sheet kraft card stock

Scissors

Scoring tool

1 sheet white card stock

Pencil

Card stock in five colors of your choice (The example uses red, orange, yellow, blue, and green.)

Craft glue

Finished card measures 5 x 7 inches (127 x 177.8 mm).

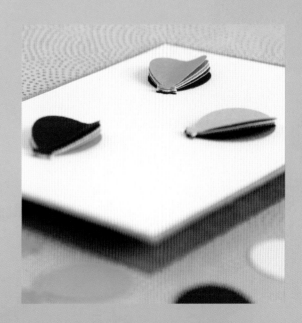

special days

you're amazing

A labor of love, "You're Amazing" was designed to help the recipient feel just how admired and appreciated they are. A higher level of detail goes into this card and it requires a steady hand; however, the creative process is satisfying and the end result is sure to impress!

designed by **Ashley Pahl**

1. Cut the kraft card stock to measure 8 x 5½ inches (203.2 x 139.7 mm). Score and fold the card stock in half widthwise, creating a card blank measuring 4 x 5½ inches (102 x 139.7 mm). Unfold.

2. On the bottom half of the unfolded card, trace the template onto what will become the front flap of the card. Make sure the design is centered.

3. Use the craft knife to follow the drawn lines. Gently erase any leftover pencil markings with a vinyl eraser.

4. Refold the card along the previously established fold line.

5. Cut the copy paper to 5¼ x 7 ¾ inches (133.35 x 196.85 mm). Fold in half.

6. Apply a thin layer of glue to the outer crease of the folded copy paper.

7. Adhere the folded paper to the inside crease of the card. It should resemble a book with pages and a cover when folded. This folded copy paper provides a white background for the paper cut lettering and acts as a liner for writing on the inside of the card.

> **TIP:** *When cutting tiny designs with a lot of detail—especially on kraft card stock—use a fresh, sharp blade with your craft knife.*

MATERIALS + TOOLS

1 sheet kraft card stock

Pencil

Craft knife with sharp blade

Self-healing cutting mat

Vinyl eraser

1 sheet white copy paper

Craft glue

Finished card measures 4 x 5½ inches (101.6 x 139.7 mm).

congratulations!

Handwritten script is back in style! This card design features my
own calligraphy, carefully translated into a paper cut template.
Paired with a hand-painted background, this card is sure
to be cherished by the recipient.

designed by **Ashley Pahl**

1. Cut the kraft card stock to measure 8 x 5½ inches (203.2 x 139.7 mm). Score and fold the kraft card stock in half widthwise, creating a card blank measuring 4 x 5½ inches (102 x 139.7 mm). Unfold.

2. On the bottom half of the unfolded card, trace the template onto what will become the front of your card. Make sure the *Congrats* text is centered.

3. Use the craft knife and cutting mat to follow the drawn lines. Gently erase any leftover pencil markings with the vinyl eraser.

4. Refold the card along the previously established fold line.

5. Cut the watercolor paper to 5¼ x 3.8 inches (133.35 x 96.52 mm). Using watercolor paints, paint stripes in a coral color as shown here or use a color of your choice.

6. When the paint is dry, apply a narrow line of craft glue to the front, top (long) edge of the watercolor paper.

7. Attach the painted paper to the inside top of the front flap of the card. The stripes should show through the cutout when the card is folded shut. Allow to dry completely (about 10 minutes).

> **TIP:** *Using heavyweight, 140 lb watercolor paper will help prevent paper from buckling.*

MATERIALS + TOOLS

1 sheet kraft card stock

Pencil

Craft knife with sharp blade

Self-healing cutting mat

Vinyl eraser

Scissors

1 sheet watercolor paper

Watercolor paints with brush and water dish

Scoring tool

Craft glue

Finished card measures 4 x 5½ inches (101.6 x 139.7 mm).

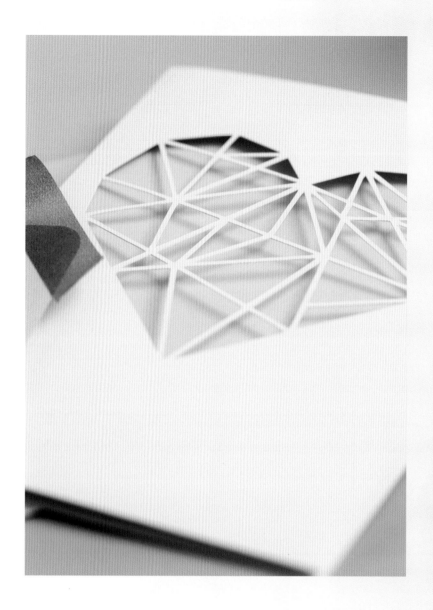

all the corners of my heart

This contemporary heart greeting card features a detailed geometric
pattern perfect for honing your paper-cutting skills. Be sure to cut
the lines as straight as possible, but be careful not to cut across
lines or you'll run the risk of cutting details away!

designed by **Sian Williams-Clarke**

1. Cut card stock to 7 x 10 inches. Score a vertical line down the middle of the white card stock and fold in half to create the card shape.

2. Trace the heart template on to the inside front flap of card. (Due to the nature of the design, you don't need to worry about the image being in reverse.)

3. Using the craft knife and cutting mat, carefully cut along the lines of the template.

4. From the colored paper, cut a square large enough to completely cover the cut out design.

5. Glue around all four edges of the right side of the colored paper. Affix colored paper to the inside (inner front flap) of the card, taking care to completely cover the cutout.

> **TIP:** *Restrict glue to only the edges of the colored paper to prevent glue from showing through the cutout of the card.*

6. Create a thin layer of glue across the white 5 × 7-inch (127 x 177.8-mm) card stock and place within the inner front flap of the card, making sure that the colored paper is entirely covered and ensuring that the edges of the card stock line up with edges of the outer card.

MATERIALS + TOOLS

2 sheets white card stock

Pencil

Craft knife

Self-healing cutting mat

1 sheet colored paper (This project uses aqua.)

Scoring tool

Glue stick

Finished card measures 5 x 7 inches (127 x 177.8 mm).

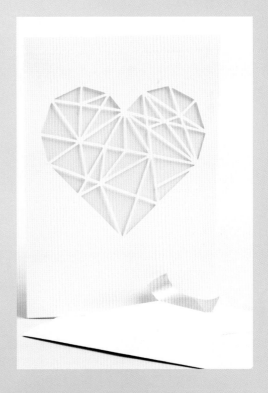

showered with love

Inspired the rainy city of Manchester, this card is a perfect way to shower your love to the recipient. This simple design requires a steady hand, and the project is good practice for your paper-cutting skills.

designed by **Sian Williams-Clarke**

1. Cut both sheets of white card stock to 5 x 7 inches (127 x 177.8 mm). Score a line widthwise down the middle of each sheet and fold in half to create the card shape. The folded cards should measure 5 x 3½ inches (127 x 88.9 mm) each. Set one sheet of card stock aside.

2. Transfer the template image on to the inner front flap of the second piece of card stock.

3. Carefully cut out the template, taking extra care along the thin lines. A metal ruler can come in handy if you aren't confident cutting very straight lines parallel to each other.

4. Using the colored paper, cut a rectangle large enough to cover the entire cut out design (around 4½ x 3 inches, 114.3 x 76.2 mm).

5. Glue around the edges of the colored paper and press onto the inside flap of card, taking care to cover the entire cutout.

6. Take the second sheet of card stock and line it up within the first, carefully aligning the scored fold.

7. Carefully glue around all four sides of the second sheet of white card stock and press it inside the outer card, creating a lining. Carefully trim any overhanging paper.

MATERIALS + TOOLS

2 sheets white card stock

Scissors

Pencil

Metal ruler (optional)

Craft knife

Self-healing cutting mat

Glue stick

1 sheet of colored paper (This project uses blue.)

Finished card measures 5 x 7 inches (127 x 177.8 mm).

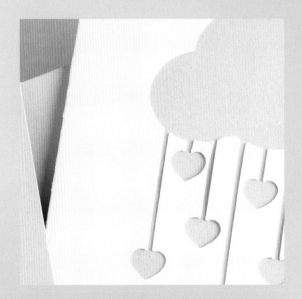

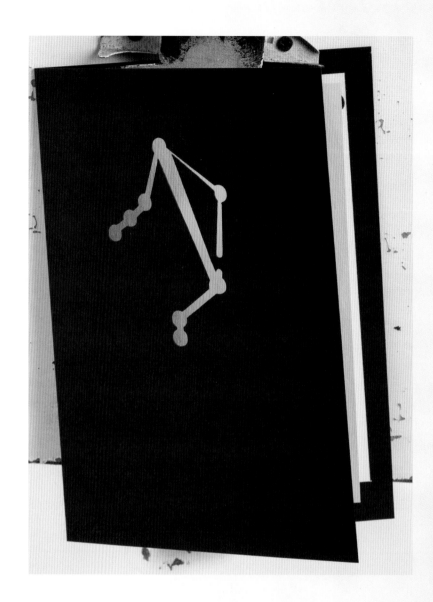

written in the stars

Inspired by horoscopes and their star constellations, this paper
cut card is perfect for any birthday throughout the year.

designed by **Sian Williams-Clarke**

1. Cut navy card stock to measure 10 x 7 inches (254 x 127.8 mm). Score and fold widthwise to create a card blank measuring 5 x 7 inches (127 x 177.8 mm).

2. Select chosen horoscope constellation, reverse the image and trace onto the inside of the card's front flap.

   TIP: *Ensure the image is reversed before cutting to guarantee image is oriented correctly on card's front.*

3. Using the craft knife and cutting mat, cut out the template.

4. Score yellow single-sided paper in half, folding to ensure that the yellow is on the outside of the fold.

5. Place glue around the edges and down the outer fold of the yellow side of paper and press into the inside of the navy stock, with fold lined up with navy card's center fold.

   TIP: *Lining up the yellow paper with the center fold inside of the navy outer card will ensure an easy opening and prevent the paper from getting creased inside the navy card.*

MATERIALS + TOOLS

1 sheet navy card stock

Pencil

Craft knife

Self-healing cutting mat

1 sheet yellow single-sided paper

Scoring tool

Glue stick

Finished card measures 5 x 7 inches (127 x 177.8 mm).

Horoscope dates are as follows:

Aries ✴ March 21–April 19

Taurus ✴ April 20–May 20

Gemini ✴ May 21–June 20

Cancer ✴ June 21–July 22

Leo ✴ July 23–August 22

Virgo ✴ August 23–September 22

Libra ✴ September 23–October 22

Scorpio ✴ October 23–November 21

Sagittarius ✴ November 22–December 21

Capricorn ✴ December 22–January 19

Aquarius ✴ January 20–February 18

Pisces ✴ February 19–March 20

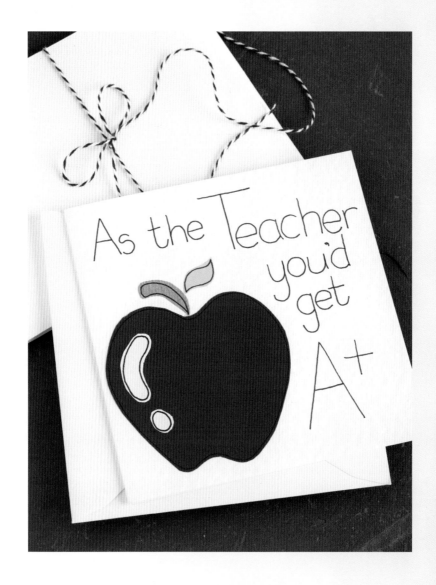

an apple a day

A handmade card is the perfect way to say "Thank you for your knowledge, your patience, and your constant smile!" Personalize this card with a favorite teacher's name, or create a stack of generic cards for each class of the day.

designed by **Louise Burgoyne**

1. Cut white card stock to 10 x 5 inches (254 x 127 mm). Score and fold widthwise down the middle of the stock to create your blank card.

2. Transfer the apple template onto the red paper, the leaf template onto the green, the stalk template onto the kraft paper, and the light reflection template onto the white paper. Once you've drawn all the shapes onto the correctly colored paper, cut them all out using scissors.

3. Trace or copy the greeting onto the top and right side of the card. You can personalize the card by adding a teacher's name or you can use a standard generic greeting of your choice.

4. Glue the apple, stalk, and leaf onto the front flap of the card as pictured. Position the white light reflection over the left side of the apple, making sure the wider part of the reflection is on top.

5. Draw an outline around each cutout shape with the fine-tip black pen.

MATERIALS + TOOLS

1 sheet white card stock

Pencil

Scissors

1 sheet red paper

1 sheet green paper

1 sheet brown kraft paper

1 sheet white paper

PVA glue or paper glue of your choice

Scoring tool

Fine-tip black pen

Finished card measures 5 x 5 inches (127 x 127 mm).

easter egg hunt

Paper piecing is one of the most fun ways to create a unique card.
Using solid card stock and a few basic craft tools, you can create
this one-of-a-kind Easter card. Fringed grass is fun for
young crafters to help create!

designed by **Margaret Beagle**

1. Cut the blue card stock to 4¾ x 5¼ inches (120.65 x 133.35 mm).

2. Using the lighter shade of green card stock, cut a strip measuring 5¼ x 1½ (133.35 x 38.1 mm). Repeat using the darker shade of green card stock. You should now have two strips, one of each shade of green.

3. Using scissors, make 1-inch (25.4 mm) deep cuts along the strips to create a 1-inch (25.4-mm) deep fringe on each green strip. These will be the grass layers.

4. Trace the larger ear template onto the white card stock twice, and the smaller ear template onto the pink card stock twice. Cut along your lines. You will have two white outer ears and two pink inner ears.

5. To assemble the card, use glue to adhere the blue card stock in the center of the kraft notecard, leaving a ¼-inch (6.35 mm) margin along each edge. Next, adhere the grass layers of the fringed green card stock. You may want to lay everything on top of the blue card stock so placement is to your liking before gluing everything down. Place the ears under the green-fringed grass and glue.

TIP: *Fringe scissors will help to make your fringe uniform and will speed up the crafting process!*

MATERIALS + TOOLS

1 sheet blue card stock

1 sheet light green card stock

1 sheet dark green card stock

1 sheet white card stock

1 sheet pink card stock

1 sheet kraft brown card stock

Scissors

Glue

Finished card measures 5 x 7 inches (127 x 177.8 mm).

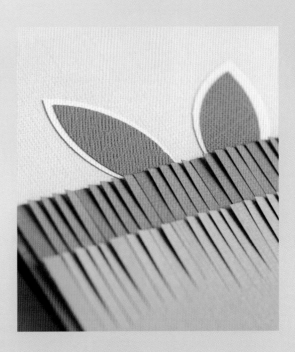

merry and bright

"May your days be merry and bright" is a warm message for the most wonderful time of the year. Cut into white or kraft card stock, this card template will allow you to make a custom set of handmade holiday cards, personalized to reflect your style.

designed by **Ashley Pahl**

1. Cut the white card stock to measure 5½ x 8 inches (139.7 x 203.2 mm). Score and fold the card stock in half widthwise, creating a card blank measuring 4 x 5½ inches (101.6 x 139.7 mm). Unfold.

2. On the bottom half of the unfolded card, transfer the template onto what will become the front of the card. Make sure the "Merry + Bright" lettering is centered on the front flap of the card in a landscape orientation.

3. Use a craft knife and cutting mat to cut along the transferred lines. Gently erase any leftover markings with a vinyl eraser.

4. Refold the card along the previously established fold line.

5. Cut the white card stock or watercolor paper to 5¼ x 3.8 inches (133.35 x 96.52 mm). Create a colorful pattern of your choice to show through the cut out lettering. Seasonal color combinations such as red, mint green, or metallics will really shine.

6. Apply a thin layer of glue to the top edge of the front of the patterned paper.

7. Adhere the patterned card stock to the inside top edge of the top flap of the card, near the crease. Allow glue to dry completely.

> **TIP:** *When creating a pattern for the background of the cut out lettering, bigger, bolder patterns like geometric shapes tend to look better than small, delicate patterns such as tiny flowers or flourishes. Geometric shapes such as lines, solid dots, and triangles tend to look less busy and make the lettering easier to read.*

MATERIALS + TOOLS

1 sheet white card stock

Craft knife with sharp blade

Self-healing cutting mat

Pencil

Vinyl eraser

Scissors

1 sheet white card stock or watercolor paper

Craft glue

Scoring tool

Markers or paints and paintbrush

Finished card measures 4 x 5½ inches (101.6 x 139.7 mm).

a visit from st. nicholas

This reindeer card takes a winter holiday icon and gives it a modern look with a simple, elegant white silhouette against a bold red background. Small rhinestones give it an extra sparkle and a satin ribbon adds some charm!

designed by **Paula Arwen Owen**

1. Cut the white card stock to 8½ x 5½ inches (215.9 x 139.7 mm). Score widthwise down the center of the card. Transfer the template to the card stock and align to the right edge, ensuring that it is aligned on what will be the front flap of the card. Cut along the transferred lines.

2. Cut the piece of red card stock slightly smaller than the whole card—about 8¼ x 5¼ inches (209.55 x 133.35 mm). Score widthwise down the middle of the stock.

3. Lay the red card stock inside of the white, ensuring that the red stock is centered within the outer card. Measure along the inside of the fold with the metal ruler, making a mark inside the fold at 1 inch (25 mm) from each edge of the card. Take your large needle and make two holes through both layers along the fold line. Thread a thin ribbon through the needle and pull it through the two holes, ensuring that the ribbon ends are outside of the card. Tie the ends of the ribbon together in a bow on the outside of the card.

4. Attach three self-stick rhinestones to the ornaments on the reindeer's antlers.

MATERIALS + TOOLS

1 sheet white card stock

Scissors

Craft knife

Self-healing cutting mat

1 sheet red card stock

Scoring tool

Metal ruler

Large needle

Thin white satin ribbon

Clear and red self-stick rhinestones, ⅛- and 1/16-inch (3.175 and 1.58 mm)

Vinyl eraser

Finished card measures 4¼ x 5½ inches (107.95 x 139.7 mm).

season's greetings

Do you want your Christmas card to stand out from the crowd this year?
Well, why not make your own for that really personal touch. These designs
are a simple and modern in design. The two designs have different
difficulty levels so when you've perfected the pattern of the tree,
you can move on to the more advanced ornament.

designed by **Sian Williams-Clarke**

1. Cut white card stock to 8 x 6 inches (203.2 x 152.4 mm), and score widthwise, creating a card measuring 4 x 6 inches (101.6 x 152.4 mm).

2. Transfer the chosen design template image onto the inside of the card. Position the template on the crease so the design is folded in half when finished. Feel free to experiment with placement.

3. Using a craft knife and cutting mat, cut along the lines of the traced template. The tree has larger sections to cut while the ornament has more intricate detail, so work slowly and carefully to ensure that you don't cut through any lines. A metal ruler can come in handy if you aren't confident about cutting very straight lines parallel to each other.

4. Working on the colored side of pearlized paper, glue around all four edges of the paper. Press onto the white outer card, ensuring that the edges line up neatly. Because this paper is single sided, the white back of the decorative paper provides the perfect canvas for writing greetings.

MATERIALS + TOOLS

1 sheet white card stock

Scorer

Pencil

Template (tree or bauble)

Craft knife

Self-healing cutting mat

Metal ruler (optional)

1 sheet colored pearlized paper (We used green for the tree design and gold for the bauble. This paper usually comes single sided.)

Glue

Finished card measures 4 x 6 inches (101.6 x 152.4 mm).

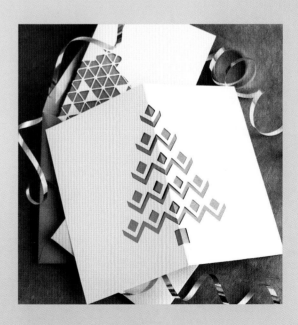

l'chaim!

Papercutting is a traditional Jewish art form. A Ketubah—or marriage certificate—is a beautiful and intricate piece of art often cut out of paper. This card uses the Star of David to create a detailed and colorful design that can be used for any Jewish Holiday. Did you know *Shalom* can mean *Peace*, *Hello*, or *Good-bye*?

designed by **Paula Arwen Owen**

1. Cut black card stock to 8½ x 5½ inches (215.9 x 139.7 mm). Score widthwise down the center of the card and fold.

2. Open the card back up and transfer the template to the card stock, ensuring that image is aligned over what will be the front flap of the card. See page xiii for transfer techniques.

3. Using a craft knife with a new blade and a cutting mat, begin cutting along the lines of the template. Go slowly and make small cuts, turning the card as needed to go around small corners and curves. Use your metal ruler to help cut the straight lines. When you have cut all the lines, you can go back over any corners or lines that need more work. Make sure the blade stays sharp; change it as soon as it starts to drag or catch too much on the paper, or if the tip breaks off.

4. Use the templates to cut out the two hexagon shapes from the gold metallic and dark blue papers.

5. Cut the blue metallic paper slightly smaller than the whole card, about 8¼ x 5¼ inches (209.55 x 133.35 mm). Score widthwise down the center of the paper.

6. Squeeze out a small amount of white glue and use a small brush to put a very thin layer of glue on the inside of the card around the two hexagon cutouts. Carefully align the gold and blue hexagon shapes over the cutouts and press down. If any glue seeps out, wipe it carefully before it dries.

7. Take the inside layer of paper and apply double-sided tape to one side. Center the paper inside the outer card and attach. Use the rubber cement eraser to gently pick up any tape that may remain on the edges.

8. Holding the card closed, center the rhinestone inside the big star and press the rhinestone down onto the inner layer of paper (through your cutout).

MATERIALS + TOOLS

1 sheet black card stock

Scissors

Craft knife

Self-healing cutting mat

1 sheet blue card stock

Metal ruler

Scoring tool

Metallic blue & gold papers

White glue

Double-sided tape

Rubber cement eraser

Small brush

³/₁₆-inch (4.76 mm) blue rhinestone

Finished card measures 4¼ x 5½ inches (107.95 x 139.7 mm).

pumpkin spice for someone nice

Autumn is the season of falling leaves, apple cider, and pumpkin spice.
This magical season was the inspiration for this card. It's perfectly
sweet for October birthdays, Halloween greetings, and
sincere notes of thankfulness. It can also serve as a
cheeky greeting for a special someone!

designed by **Ashley Pahl**

1. Cut the white card stock to measure 5½ x 8 inches (139.7 x 203.2 mm). Score and fold the card stock in half widthwise, creating a card blank measuring 4 x 5½ inches (101.6 x 139.7 mm). Unfold.

2. On the bottom half of the unfolded card, transfer the template onto what will become the front of the card. Make sure the pumpkin is centered on the front flap of the card.

3. Use the craft knife to follow the transferred line. Gently erase any leftover markings using a vinyl eraser.

4. Refold the card along the previously established fold line.

5. Cut the orange card stock or paper to 5¼ x 3.8 inches (133.35 x 96.52 mm).

6. Apply a narrow line of craft glue to the front, top (long) edge of the orange paper.

7. Attach the orange paper to the inside top of the front flap of the card. Allow glue to dry completely (about 10 minutes).

> **TIP:** *If you have difficulty cutting a straight thin line (such as the lines that hold the text in this card) on card stock, a ruler might be helpful. Hold the ruler against the penciled line and allow your craft knife to rest against the ruler as a guide.*

MATERIALS + TOOLS

1 sheet white card stock

Pencil

Craft knife

Self-healing cutting mat

Vinyl eraser

Scissors

1 sheet orange card stock or paper

Scoring tool

Craft glue

Finished card measures 4 x 5½ inches (101.6 x 139.7 mm).

blank cards

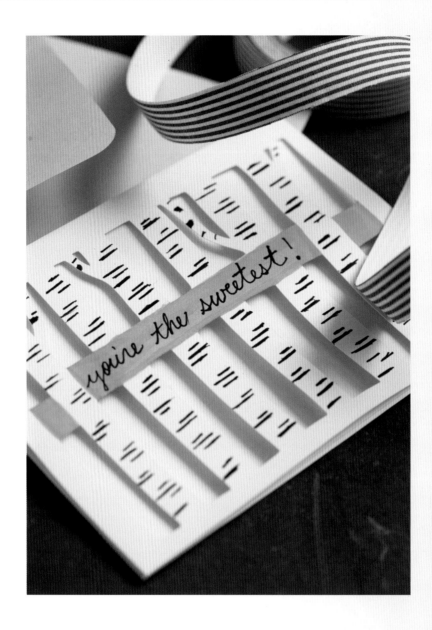

birch

A birch tree forest evokes a quiet, peaceful ambience, and it's beautiful
throughout all four seasons. By changing the color of the banner
and the wording, this card can be used for holidays,
birthdays, baby showers, weddings, and more!

designed by **Ashley Pahl**

1. Cut the white card stock to measure 8 x 5½ inches (203.2 x 139.7 mm). Score and fold the card stock in half widthwise, creating a card blank measuring 4 x 5½ inches (101.6 x 139.7 mm). Unfold.

2. On the bottom half of the unfolded card, transfer the template onto what will become the front flap of the card. Make sure the birch trees are centered on the front flap of the card.

3. Use the craft knife and cutting mat to follow the transferred lines. Gently erase any leftover markings with a vinyl eraser.

4. Use either watercolor or acrylic paints to paint the banner a solid color. Add depth to the design by letting the banner "weave" through some of the trees by leaving some of the banner white where a tree is present.

5. Use black paint or the felt-tipped pen to draw black lines on the birch trees. You can add as many or as few as you would like.

6. When banner paint is completely dry (about 10 minutes), write your message on the banner in black ink.

7. After all the paint and ink has dried, refold the card along the previously established fold line.

8. Cut the copy paper to 5¼ x 7¾ inches (133.35 x 196.85 mm). Fold in half.

9. Apply a thin layer of glue to the upper edge of the copy paper, near the fold.

10. Adhere the folded paper to the inside back flap of the card along the crease. It should resemble a book with pages and a cover when folded. This folded copy paper provides a white background for the paper cut trees and also acts as a liner for writing on the inside of the card.

MATERIALS + TOOLS

1 sheet white card stock, 8 x 5½ inches (203.2 x 139.7 mm)

Pencil

Craft knife

Self-healing cutting mat

Vinyl eraser

Paints (watercolor or acrylic), colors of your choice (Red, green, and yellow were used for this project.)

Paintbrush

Black felt-tip marker or pen

Scissors

1 sheet white copy paper

Scoring tool

Craft glue

Finished card measures 4 x 5½ inches (101.6 x 139.7 mm).

TIP: *Before writing your message on the painted banner, plan the message out on a scrap of paper. This allows you to better judge the placement as well as the styling of the words.*

shoot for the stars

This arrow note card is a perfect introduction card to paper-cut greeting
cards. The design is simple, clean, and open-ended. This note
card can be used for almost any occasion, from Valentine's
Day to birthdays, weddings, or "just because."

designed by **Ashley Pahl**

1. Cut the kraft card stock to measure 8 x 5½ inches (203.2 x 139.7 mm). Score and fold the card stock in half widthwise, creating a card blank measuring 4 x 5½ inches (101.6 x 139.7 mm). Unfold.

2. Transfer the template onto what will be the front of the card (the bottom half of the unfolded card). Make sure the arrow is centered.

3. Use the craft knife and cutting mat to follow the penciled line. Gently erase any leftover pencil markings with a vinyl eraser.

4. Refold the card along the previously established fold line.

5. Cut the glittered card stock to 5¼ x 3¾ inches (133.35 x 95.25 mm). Working from the front of the stock, apply a thin, steady line of hot glue along the top edge of the sheet.

6. Attach the glitter card stock to the inside top of the front flap of the card (just below the fold) while the glue is still hot. The glitter card stock should now be showing through the arrow silhouette when the card is folded shut. Allow to dry completely (about 10 minutes).

> **TIP:** *You can use your own creative eye to choose different backgrounds for Step 6—from solid matte colors to patterned or textured papers.*

MATERIALS + TOOLS

1 sheet kraft card stock

Pencil

Craft knife with sharp blade

Self-healing cutting mat

Vinyl eraser

Scissors

Scoring tool

Silver glittered card stock sheet

Hot glue gun with glue sticks

Finished card measures 4 x 5½ inches (101.6 x 139.7 mm).

I like you a latte

Who doesn't love the surprise of a handwritten piece of snail mail from a loved one? This "Let's Get Coffee" card is a thoughtful gesture to stay in touch and a friendly invitation to catch up. It's the perfect note card for old friends and new flames alike.

designed by **Ashley Pahl**

1. Cut the white card stock to measure 8 x 5½ inches (203.2 x 139.7 mm). Score and fold the card stock in half widthwise, creating a card blank measuring 4 x 5½ inches (101.6 x 139.7 mm). Unfold.

2. On the bottom half of the unfolded card, transfer the template onto what will become the front flap of the card. Make sure the coffee cup is centered on the front flap.

3. Use the craft knife and cutting mat to follow the transferred line. Gently erase any leftover markings using a vinyl eraser.

4. Use either watercolor or acrylic paints to paint the words brown, and the heart a color of your choice.

5. After the paint has dried completely (about 10 minutes), refold the card along the previously established fold line.

6. Cut the copy paper to 5¼ x 7¾ inches (133.35 x 196.85 mm). Fold in half.

7. Apply a thin layer of glue to the upper edge of the copy paper near the fold.

8. Adhere the folded paper to the inner back flap of the card, along the crease. It should resemble a book with pages and a cover when folded. This folded copy paper provides a white background for the lettering and heart and acts as a liner for writing on the inside of the card.

> **TIP:** *Cutting small lettering can be tricky. To avoid cutting mistakes, try cutting card stock in short, shallow stabbing motions around the letters rather than long, constant slices.*

MATERIALS + TOOLS

1 sheet white card stock

Pencil

Craft knife

Self-healing cutting mat

Vinyl eraser

Paints (watercolor or acrylic) and paintbrush

Scissors

1 sheet white copy paper

Scoring tool

Craft glue

Finished card measures 4 x 5½ inches (101.6 x 139.7 mm).

thanks much

This gradient thank you card is simple to make. The instructions demonstrate the method of using brush pens to achieve the gradient color look, but why not experiment with using different colored papers to introduce new shades, patterns, and textures?

designed by **Sian Williams-Clarke**

1. Score a line widthwise across the middle of the 7 x 10-inch (177.8 x 254-mm) white card stock and fold in half to create the card shape.

2. Transfer the template image onto the inside of the card's front flap, aligning template against the card's bottom edge.

3. Using a craft knife and cutting mat, cut along the lines of the template.

4. Cut out one rectangle from the colored paper to fit over the bottom "thank you," leaving enough space around the edges to be able to glue the paper behind the cutout—about 1½ x 4½ inches (38.1 x 114.3 mm). Using the darker shade of brush pen, color over the entire pink rectangle.

5. Place a thin line of glue around the edges of the colored paper and attach to the inside front flap of the card, covering the cut out "Thank You" closest to the bottom edge of the white card.

6. Cut out a second rectangle from the colored paper to fit over the bottom two "Thank You" cutouts, about 2¼ x 4½ inches (57.15 x 114.3 mm).

7. Using the lighter shade of the brush pen, color in the entire sheet (the second rectangle of colored paper).

8. Place a thin line of glue around the edges of the colored paper and attach to the inside front flap of the card, covering both "Thank You" cutouts closest to the bottom edge of the white card.

9. Cut out a rectangle from the colored paper large enough to fit over the entire template, about 3¼ x 4½ inches (82.55 x 114.3 mm).

10. Glue the edges and fix over the entire cutout template.

11. Cover the entire back of the inner flap of the card with the 5 x 7-inch (127 x 177.8 mm) white card stock, ensuring the pieces line up neatly. Make sure that all of the pink paper is covered.

MATERIALS + TOOLS

Scoring tool

1 sheet white card stock

Pencil

Craft knife

Self-healing cutting mat

Scissors

1 sheet colored paper (This project uses pink.)

Brush pens in two shades of pink

Glue stick

1 sheet white card stock

Finished card measures 5 x 7 inches (127 x 177.8 mm).

floating on a calm sea

When life's waters get rocky, it's nice to have a partner to support you through the storm. Thank those who stick with you through thick and thin with this nautical card. Hand stitching and fun ribbons give you an opportunity to explore your sewing chest as well as your paper stash!

designed by **Nikki Meara**

1. Cut both sheets of white card stock to measure 10 x 5 inches (254 x 127 mm). Score and fold the card stock in half widthwise, creating a card blank measuring 5 x 5 inches (127 x 127 mm). Unfold. Set one piece of card stock aside.

2. Transfer the sailboat and waves template onto the inside front of the second piece of card stock.

3. Use a craft knife and cutting mat to carefully cut out the sailboat shape. Use a metal ruler to ensure lines are parallel and boats line up.

4. Using a needle, make small and evenly-spaced holes approximately 3/16 inch (4.76 mm) apart along the wave shape that you have transferred. Starting from the inside of the card, sew along the wave pattern, threading through the holes. Tape the ends of the thread on the inside of the card.

5. Cut a length of each of the ribbons (long enough to cover the cut sailboats) and stick them in place with transparent cellulose tape behind the sailboat shapes. Start with the red stripe for the hull of the boats and the green ribbon for the flags. Finally, place the blue ribbons for the sails.

6. Take the second blank card and, using a craft knife, cutting mat, and metal ruler, cut the card in half along the fold. Stick double-sided tape along the four edges of the halved square of the card and use this to back the inside of the greeting card. Stick the backing card 1/16 inch (1.6 mm) away from the fold to ensure the card closes properly.

7. Using the craft knife, cutting mat, and metal ruler, trim any paper or ribbon that hangs over the edges of the card.

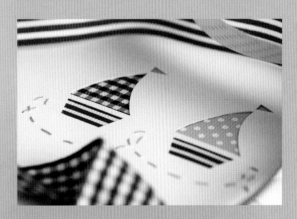

a happy little note

This "happy" card combines the beauty of hand lettering with the exciting process of paper cutting. "Happy" is the perfect card to make and have ready-to-go for any joyous occasion.

designed by **Ashley Pahl**

1. Cut the kraft card stock to measure 8 x 5½ inches (203.2 x 139.7 mm). Score and fold the card stock in half widthwise, creating a card blank measuring 4 x 5½ inches (101.6 x 139.7 mm). Unfold.

2. On the bottom half of the unfolded card, transfer the template onto what will become the front flap of the card. Make sure the *happy* text is centered.

3. Use the craft knife and cutting mat to follow the transferred line. Gently erase any leftover markings with the vinyl eraser.

4. Refold the card along the previously established fold line.

5. Cut the copy paper to 5¼ x 7¾ inches (133.35 x 196.85 mm). Fold in half.

6. Apply a thin layer of glue to the back top edge of the copy paper, near the fold.

7. Adhere the folded paper to the inside bottom flap of the card, along the crease. It should resemble a book with pages and a cover when folded. This folded copy paper provides not only a white background for the paper-cut lettering, but also acts as a liner for writing on the inside of the card.

> **TIP:** *When using thinner paper such as copy paper, a ballpoint or brush-tip glue pen is a great choice for a thin, smooth application.*

MATERIALS + TOOLS

1 sheet Kraft card stock

Pencil

Craft knife

Self-healing cutting mat

Vinyl eraser

Scissor

1 sheet white copy paper

Craft glue

Finished card measures 4 x 5½ inches (101.6 x 139.7 mm).

it's heart to resist you

There are many occasions that can cause you to feel overwhelmed with love and joy: weddings, graduations, first driving lessons, or even just a regular "I Love You." This card, overflowing with hearts, conveys the sentiment "I am overwhelmed with love for you!"

designed by **Mia Yoshihara-Bradshaw**

1. Using a paper cutter, cut white card stock to 8 x 5½ inches (203.2 x 139.7 mm). Score widthwise and fold in half, creating a 5½ x 4-inch (139.7 x 101.6-mm) card.

2. Using a paper cutter, cut the pink textured card stock to 8 x 5½ inches (203.2 x 139.7 mm). Trim the shorter edges slightly so that the stock is just smaller than the white card stock, about 7.9 x 5.4 inches (200.66 mm x 137.16 mm). Score widthwise and fold in half. Set aside.

3. Unfold the white card stock and lay the card on the cutting mat. Transfer the heart template to the front flap of the card, making sure that the template is centered.

4. Open the card flat so the heart design is at the top of the card. Apply double-sided tape just below the inner fold so that you can attach the pink inner card.

5. Position the pink inner card within the white card stock, ensuring that the creases align.

6. Apply the pink inner card to the double-sided tape by pressing firmly.

7. Flip the card over and fold. Place the card under heavy weight such as a thick book to help the card lay flat.

MATERIALS + TOOLS

Guillotine paper cutter

1 sheet white card stock

1 sheet pink textured card stock

Craft knife

Self-healing cutting mat

Pencil

Heart template

Double-sided tape

Scoring tool

Finished card measures 4 x 5 1/2 inches (101.6 x 139.7 mm).

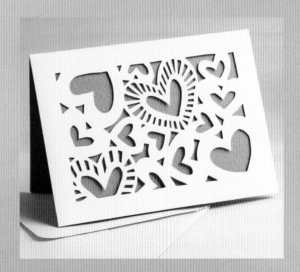

you are my favorite

Everybody has a favorite person—who is yours? This charming
note card is easy to customize with painted color
so that it suits the recipient perfectly.

designed by **Ashley Pahl**

1. Cut the white card stock to measure 8 x 5½ inches (203.2 x 139.7 mm). Score and fold the card stock in half widthwise, creating a card blank measuring 4 x 5½ inches (101.6 x 139.7 mm). Unfold.

2. On the bottom half of the unfolded card, transfer the template onto what will become the front flap of the card. Make sure the "You Are My Favorite" text is centered on the front flap of the card.

3. Use the craft knife and cutting mat to follow the transferred line. Gently erase any leftover markings using a vinyl eraser.

4. Use either watercolor or acrylic paints to paint over the words. Paint all of the words the same color or select a different color of paint for each line of text. Let the paint dry completely (about 10 minutes).

5. After the paint has dried (about 10 minutes), refold the card along the previously established fold line.

6. Cut the copy paper to 5¼ x 7¾ inches (133.35 x 196.85 mm). Fold in half.

7. Apply a thin layer of glue to the upper edge of the folded copy paper, near the fold.

8. Adhere the folded paper to the inside bottom flap of the card along the crease. It should resemble a book with pages and a cover when folded. This folded copy paper provides a white background for the paper cut lettering, but also acts as a liner for writing on the inside of the card.

TIP: *When using multiple paint colors, paint a swatch of each color on a scrap of paper to ensure that you like the color combination before applying to the card.*

a trunkful of balloons

This cheery elephant carries festive greetings and one bright balloon!
Choose different combinations of ribbon and felt to modify this
card and it can transform from a child's birthday card
to a grown-up's heartfelt note.

designed by **Nikki Meara**

1. Cut both sheets of card stock to 5 x 10 inches (254 x 127 mm). Score widthwise and fold, creating two cards measuring 5 x 5 inches (127 x 127 mm). Set one card aside.

2. On the other piece of card stock, transfer the elephant template onto the inner front flap of the card. Make sure the elephant is slightly smaller than the width of the ribbon.

3. Using a craft knife and cutting mat, carefully cut the shape of the elephant.

4. Use a glue stick to adhere the ribbon to the inside of the card behind the elephant cutout. Secure the edges of the ribbon with transparent cellulose tape.

5. Pick up the second blank card and, using a craft knife, cutting mat, and metal ruler, cut the card in half along the fold. Place double-sided tape along the four edges of the halved square of card and use this to back the inside of the greeting card. Stick the backing card $1/16$ inch (1.6 mm) away from the fold to ensure the card closes properly.

6. Using the craft knife, cutting mat, and metal ruler, trim any ribbon or paper that hangs over the edges of the card.

7. Use a fine-tip black pen to draw the elephant's tail hairs and balloon string.

8. With a hole punch and some scrap white card, cut out an eye for the elephant. Draw a black dot in the middle with the fine line pen and stick the eye on the elephant with a tiny glue dot.

9. Cut out a rounded ear shape from the red felt and attach it with a glue dot.

10. Adhere the button balloon on the end of the string with a glue dot.

MATERIALS + TOOLS

2 sheets white card stock

Scoring tool

Pencil

Craft knife

Self-healing cutting mat

Glue stick

Patterned ribbon or a strip of fabric at least $5/8$ inch (15.87 mm) wide

Transparent cellulose tape

Metal ruler

Double-sided tape

Fine-tip black pen

Hole punch

Glue dots ($1/8$ & $3/8$ inch; 3.17 & 9.525 mm) or glue gun

Scissors

Red felt

1 decorative button

Finished card measures 5 x 5 inches (127 x 127 mm).

key to my heart

This Valentine's Day card has a vintage look with brown and cream recycled paper, a distressed pattern, and a plush velvet heart. Give someone the key to your heart with this multi-layered card!

designed by **Paula Arwen Owen**

1. Cut the cream card stock to 8½ x 5½ inches (215.9 x 139.7 mm). Score and fold the stock widthwise in half.

2. Transfer the template onto the card stock, ensuring that the template is aligned over what will be the front flap of the card. Using the craft knife and cutting mat, carefully cut along the lines of the template.

4. Cut the brown card stock to 8¼ x 5¼ inches (209.55 x 133.35 mm). Score and fold the stock widthwise in half. Use the templates to cut the rectangular opening out of the brown card stock, aligning the template with the right edge. Cut the heart shape from the red velvet paper. Set aside.

5. Cut the patterned paper slightly smaller than the brown layer, about 8 x 5 inches (203.2 x 139.7 mm). Score and fold the paper widthwise, in half. Set aside.

6. Squeeze out a small amount of white glue and use a small brush to paint a very thin layer of glue on the inside of the card around the heart opening. Carefully align the velvet heart and press it down. If any glue seeps out, wipe it carefully before it dries.

7. Take the inside layer of brown card stock and apply double-sided tape to one side. Line it up with the inside of the card and the design and attach. Do the same with the patterned paper, aligning it inside the brown card stock. Use the rubber cement eraser to gently pick up any tape that may remain on the edges.

MATERIALS + TOOLS

1 sheet cream card stock

Scissors

Scoring tool

Pencil

Craft knife

Self-healing cutting mat

Metal ruler

1 sheet brown card stock

Red velvet paper

Patterned paper of your choosing

White glue

Small paintbrush

Double-sided tape

Rubber cement eraser

Finished card measures 4¼ x 5½ inches (107.95 x 139.7 mm).

sew your garden

Say it with flowers! Paper-cut petals and buttons combine to make
a simple and beautiful card for any occasion.

designed by **Nikki Meara**

1. Cut both sheets of card stock to 5 x 10 inches (127 x 254 mm). Score widthwise and fold, creating two cards measuring 5 x 5 inches (127 x 127 mm). Set one card aside.

2. Transfer the template onto the front flap of the second piece of card stock.

3. Using the craft knife and cutting mat, cut the marked petals almost to the ends near the button circles. Do not cut them out completely.

4. Close the card and carefully fold up the petals of the flower from the front of the card.

5. Cut out three squares of different colored paper. Make sure they are slightly bigger than the flowers, approximately 2½ x 2½ inches (63.5 x 63.5 mm). Place each square of paper over a flower on the inside of the card using transparent cellulose tape. Ensure that one color does not overlap with a neighboring flower.

6. Take the second blank card and, using a craft knife, cutting mat, and metal ruler, cut the card in half along the fold. Place double-sided tape along the four edges of the halved square of the card and use this to back the inside of the greeting card. Stick the backing card ¹⁄₁₆ inch (1.6 mm) away from the fold to ensure that the card closes properly.

7. Using the craft knife, cutting mat, and metal ruler, trim any paper that hangs over the edges of the card.

8. Place the three buttons in the center of each flower using glue dots.

MATERIALS + TOOLS

Two sheets white card stock

Pencil

Craft knife

Self-healing cutting mat

Scissors

3 pieces of colored paper or origami paper

Transparent cellulose tape

Metal ruler

Double-sided tape

3 colored buttons

Scoring tool

Double-sided adhesive dots, ³⁄₈ inch (9.52 mm)

Finished card measures 5 x 5 inches (127 x 127 mm).

sail away with me

This card captures the essence of a cool breeze on sparkling blue waters as a sailboat glides by under clear skies. Vellum paper gives a translucent glow to the design. This is a great summer card for Father's Day, a birthday, or any breezy occasion.

designed by **Paula Arwen Owen**

1. Cut both sheets of card stock down to 8½ x 5½ inches (215.9 x 139.7 mm). Score the stock widthwise down the center of the card.

2. Transfer the template onto the card stock, aligned to the right edge, ensuring that the template is centered over what will be the front flap of the card.

3. Using a craft knife with a new blade and the cutting knife, cut along the lines of the template. Go slowly and make small cuts, turning the card as needed to go around small corners and curves. Use the metal ruler to help cut the straight lines. When all the lines are cut, go back over any corners or lines that need more work. Make sure the blade stays sharp; change it as soon as it starts to drag or catch too much on the paper, or if the tip breaks off.

4. Cut a piece of vellum to 4 x 2¾ inches (101.6 x 69.85 mm). Cut a piece of metallic blue paper to 4 x 2 3/8 (101.6 x 60.32 mm). Cut the other piece of white card stock slightly smaller than the whole card, to about 8¼ x 5¼ inches (209.55 x 133.35 mm).

5. Turn the card upside down and measure to the center where it will fold in half. Score along the inside of the card, using a scoring tool. Fold the card and press down to get a nice clean edge.

6. Repeat Step 5 with the inside layer of the white card stock.

7. Take the vellum paper and apply a small amount of double-sided tape to the edges. A tape roller works well for this. Attach the vellum piece to the inside of the card for the sky. Do the same to the dark blue paper and attach to the inside of the card for the water.

8. Take the inside layer of the card stock and apply tape to one side. Line it up with the inside of the card and attach. Use the rubber cement eraser to gently pick up any tape that may remain on the edges.

MATERIALS + TOOLS

2 sheets white card stock

Scissors

Scoring tool

Pencil

Craft knife

Self-healing cutting mat

Metal ruler

1 sheet vellum paper

1 sheet metallic blue paper

Double-sided tape

Rubber cement eraser

Finished card measures 4¼ x 5½ inches (107.95 x 139.7 mm).

a rosy outlook

Roses are known for their rich colors, velvety petals, and luxurious scent.
This greeting card celebrates the uniqueness of yellow roses, but
you can choose any color for your flower blossoms!

designed by **Mia Yoshihara-Bradshaw**

1. Using a paper cutter, cut white card stock to 8 x 5½ inches (203.2 x 139.7 mm). Score widthwise and fold in half, creating a 5½ x 4-inch (139.7 x 101.6-mm) card.

2. Using a paper cutter, cut the gray card stock to 8 x 5½ inches (203.2 x 139.7 mm). Trim the shorter edges slightly so that the stock is just smaller than the white card stock, about 7.9 x 5.4 (200.66 mm x 137.16 mm). Score widthwise and fold in half. Set aside.

3. Unfold the white card stock and lay the card on the cutting mat. Transfer the template to the front flap of the card, making sure that the template is centered. Cut out the template, starting with the smaller details and working up to the larger cutouts.

4. Cut two pieces of yellow paper that are approximately the same shape and size of each rose. Attach the yellow paper behind each rose with glue, so that the yellow color shows through the cutout areas.

5. Flip over the card so that the cutout design is at the top of the card. Apply double-sided tape just below the inner fold so that you can attach the gray inner card.

6. Position the gray inner card within the white card stock, ensuring that the creases align.

7. Apply the gray inner card to the double-sided tape by pressing firmly.

8. Flip the card over and fold. Place the card under heavy weight such as a thick book to help the card lay flat.

MATERIALS + TOOLS

1 sheet white card stock

Guillotine paper cutter

Scoring tool

1 sheet gray card stock

Craft knife

Self-healing cutting mat

Pencil

Rose template

Scissors

1 sheet yellow card stock

Glue stick

Double-sided tape

Finished card measures 4 x 5½ inches (101.6 x 139.7 mm).

templates

Photocopy at 100%.

It's a  Girl

It's a Boy

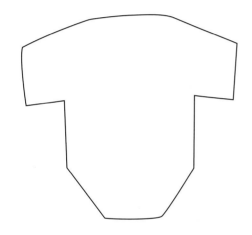

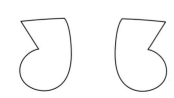

Photocopy at 100%.

Photocopy at 100%.

Photocopy at 125% to enlarge.

Mr
& Mr

Mr
& Mrs

Mrs
& Mrs

Photocopy at 100%.

Happy
New Year

Photocopy at 100%.

Photocopy at 100%.

conGRADulations

Photocopy at 100%.

BEST DAD EVER

many adventures *page 22*

Photocopy at 100%.

you're amazing *page 26*

Photocopy at 100%.

Congrats

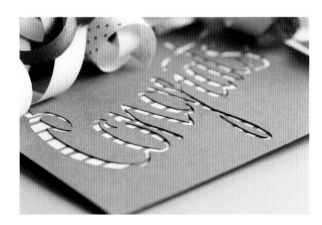

Photocopy at 100%.

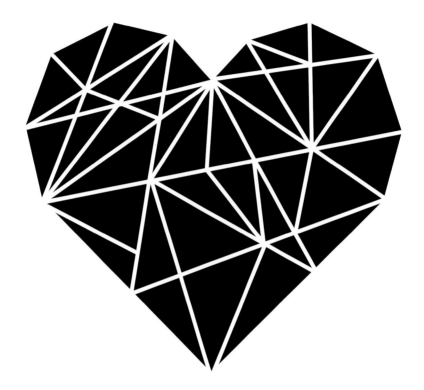

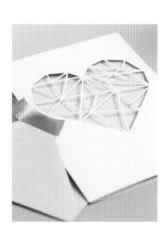

Photocopy at 100%.

written in the stars *page 34*

Photocopy at 125% to enlarge.

Horoscope dates are as follows:

Aries ✶ March 21–April 19

Taurus ✶ April 20–May 20

Gemini ✶ May 21–June 20

Cancer ✶ June 21–July 22

Leo ✶ July 23–August 22

Virgo ✶ August 23–September 22

Libra ✶ September 23–October 22

Scorpio ✶ October 23–November 21

Sagittarius ✶ November 22–December 21

Capricorn ✶ December 22–January 19

Aquarius ✶ January 20–February 18

Pisces ✶ February 19–March 20

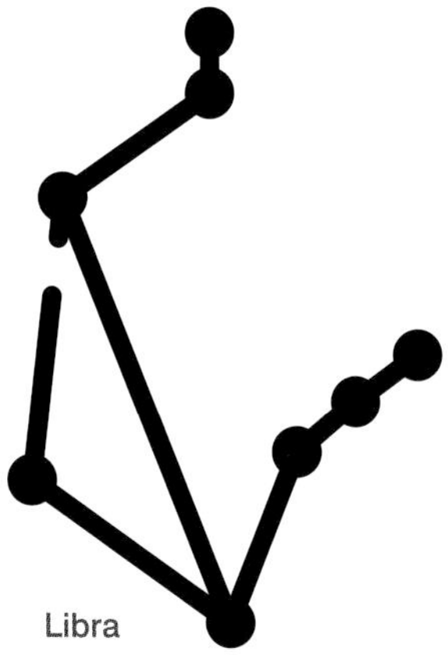

Libra

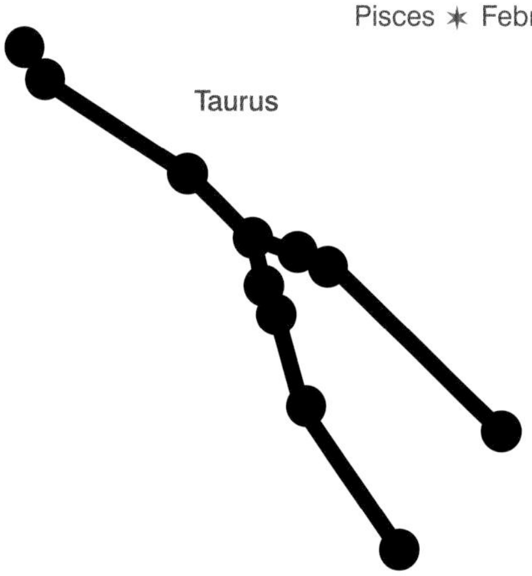

Taurus

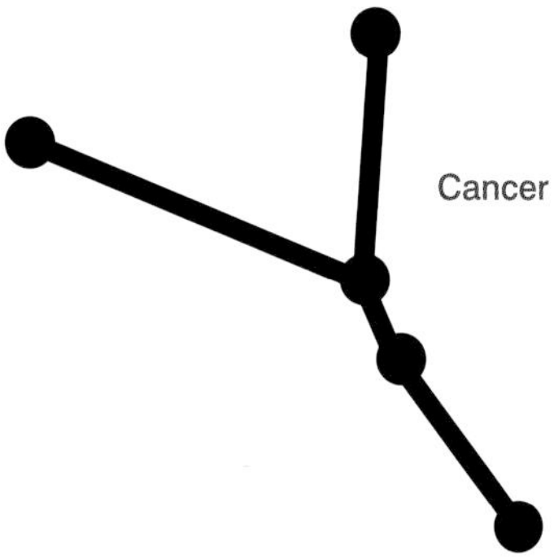

Cancer

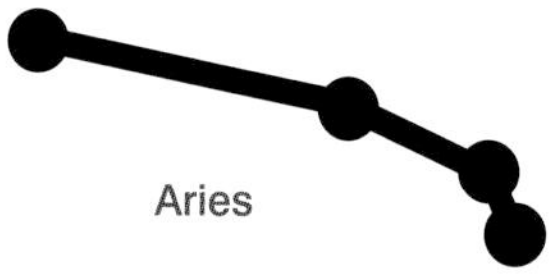

Aries

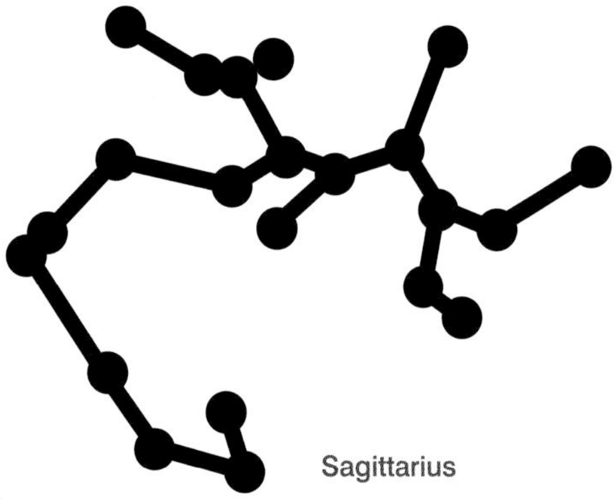

Sagittarius

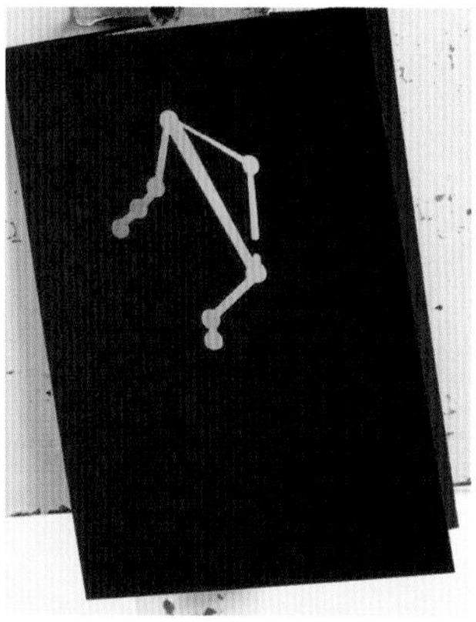

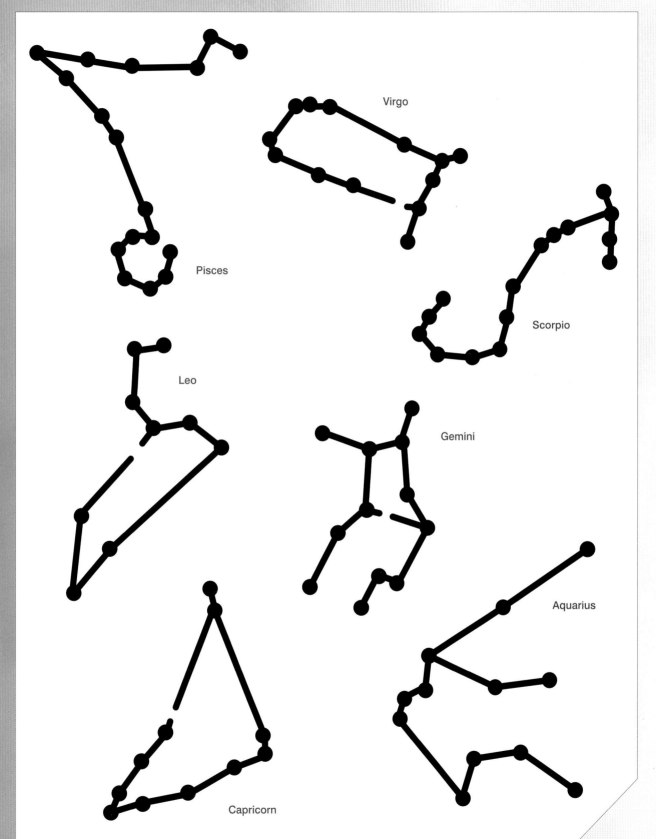

Virgo

Pisces

Scorpio

Leo

Gemini

Aquarius

Capricorn

93

Photocopy at 100%.

As the Teacher you'd get A+

easter egg hunt *page 38*

Photocopy at 100%.

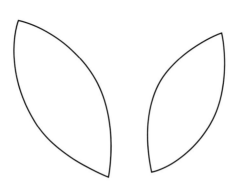

merry and bright *page 40*

MERRY
+BRIGHT

Photocopy at 100%.

Photocopy at 100%.

Photocopy at 100%.

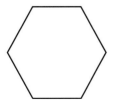

Photocopy at 100%.

Photocopy at 100%.

shoot for the stars *page 54*

Photocopy at 100%.

I like you a latte *page 56*

Photocopy at 100%.

Photocopy at 100%.

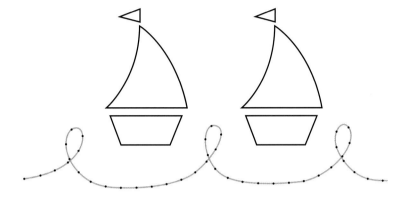

Photocopy at 100%.

Photocopy at 100%.

Photocopy at 100%.

Photocopy at 100%.

Photocopy at 100%.

Photocopy at 100%.

Photocopy at 100%.

Photocopy at 100%.

Designer Biographies

Paula Arwen Owen is an artist who works in hand-cut paper silhouettes and collage, combining simple, elegant lines against tapestries of texture and color to create compelling illustrations.

A graduate of Parsons School of Design, Paula has years of experience in illustration and graphic design. Her illustration work has appeared on many book covers, magazines, and apparel. Her greeting cards have been featured on several well-known blogs.

Paula lives at the edge of an enchanted forest in the Catskill Mountains with her husband and a variety of creatures—domestic, wild, and mythical. Paula's unique cut-paper greeting cards, artwork, and decals are available at her Etsy shop—www.etsy.com/shop/arwendesigns—and in retail stores.

Margaret Beagle has been hooked on paper since shopping for school supplies in kindergarten. She is the creator of Rainy Day Colors, a shop of cheerful handmade goods. Her days are full of coffee drinking, toddler wrangling, and paper cutting.

Louise Burgoyne grew up in the beautiful English countryside of Shropshire. With a natural artistic ability she was always interested in arts and crafts. Inspired by her late mother, Louise gained a Bachelor's Honour degree in 3D design, specializing in Ceramics. She worked for many years as a professional ceramic artist; but upon moving to Nottingham she found it just wasn't feasible to take her kiln with her, so she needed a craft that she could make on a dining table and wasn't too expensive to start. She began to design her handmade cards using just colored papers, glue, scissors, and a pen, often adorning her designs with recycled materials found around her home. Now Louise designs and makes all her own cards. She believes that the simplicity of the designs is what makes her cards truly affective, finding inspiration in everything around her, especially her loved ones.

Louise has sold her work to numerous retail shops and at craft fairs across the United Kingdom, and she now sells her work around the world via her Etsy shop, which can be found at www.etsy.com/shop/SamfireGreetingCards.

Ashley Pahl is a painter, stationery designer, and blogger who lives in East Lansing, Michigan. Using her background of an earth sciences degree from Michigan State University and frequent visits to the local botanical gardens as inspiration, most of Ashley's work includes themes from nature or natural textures. Ashley founded her handmade stationery business in 2007 and has since been featured in publications such as *I Heart Stationery* by Charlotte Rivers; *Simply Handmade Magazine*; *The Huffington Post*; *Apartment Therapy*; *The Etsy Blog* as a contributor and featured seller; and many more. You can find Ashley's work online at www.AshleyPahl.com.

Sian Williams-Clarke grew up in an artistic family and was encouraged to explore and discover a variety of techniques from textiles to photography. She completed a fashion course at Manchester City College and held a place on the Art and Design Foundation at Manchester Metropolitan University. In 2011, Sian returned to crafting. Inspired by artists such as Paper Panda and Rob Ryan, she began paper cutting, ultimately transitioning into freelance work. Alongside her prints and originals—which include hand illustrated and hand-cut original art pieces ranging from geometrical shapes to fairy-tale inspired pieces—Sian sells a range of paper-cut greeting cards, which can be found in a number of art shops and online under her brand name Crafts By Sian. She can be found at Etsy under the name CraftsBySian, and her work is sold at The Fox Fairy, Darby's Art Café, and the Torrs Art Café.

Amanda Sueiro Rier is a graphic designer with a love for good typography, bold color and, of course, paper goods! She has a BFA in Graphic Design from Barry University and a Post Baccalaureate certificate from the School of the Museum of Fine Art in Boston. Amanda started her stationery company, PaperBird, as a way to express her creativity and to share her love of paper goods with others. Amanda lives in sunny West Palm Beach, Florida, with her husband and two cats. When she isn't designing, painting, or sharpening her photography skills, she can be found out by the pool, in the kitchen baking, or at Disney World!

Brita Vallens is an Assistant Editor at Lark Crafts. She loves to doodle and craft—especially with paper. Give her a piece of paper and a pen, and she'll happily doodle away for hours. Most recently, she has been experimenting with doodle cutouts, made by cutting intricate designs out of paper using a utility knife. You can find her blogging at LarkCrafts.com and crafting all over Manhattan.

Mia Yoshihara-Bradshaw is a graphic designer and self-taught paper-cutting artist living in Seattle, Washington. She graduated with a BFA in design from Western Washington University. Mia's art combines elements of traditional Japanese paper-cutting (kiri-e), silhouettes, and mixed-media collage. Similar to kiri-e, her process involves meticulous attention to detail. Utilizing a razor, silhouettes and patterns are carefully carved to define the form. The piece is then brought to life through a collage of chiyogami paper, ribbon, and other materials. Mia's art is regularly shown in exhibitions in the Seattle area. In addition to exhibitions, she has given lectures and demonstrations on paper-cutting and conducted adult and children's workshops. Her work is available online at miayoshihara.com and in several retail shops in the Seattle area.

Index